"In a world that threatens our daily extinction, I race quicksilver to the ephemera made flesh in the sensoria dreamed by Juan Ramón Jiménez, Alfonso Reyes, Antonio Machado, Gabriela Mistral, Sor Juana, Ernesto Cardenal—and Harold Recinos. In his poems, imperious walls violently divide and tears of loss and unbelonging lacerate souls. Yet again this wordsmith extraordinaire jolts us back alive to the power of our life force: creativity, curiosity, and fellowship!"

—FREDERICK LUIS ALDAMA, Ohio State University

"*After Dark*, while presented as a poetry collection, is better understood as liturgy. Open this book and let love lift you up and break your heart. Through his achingly beautiful words, Harold Recinos asks that his readers labor for justice to remake American society—a society that has failed to meet the basic human needs of too many of our Latino sisters and brothers, especially their precious children, our precious children."

—LORI MARIE CARLSON, author of *Cool Salsa, Red Hot Salsa* and *The Sunday Tertulia*

"Protest poetry is deliberate and unafraid in the capable hands of Harold Recinos. In this collection you will hear an authentic poet possessing a quintessential American voice that echoes with Langston, Piñero, and Angelou, all shouting, 'This is what you have killed, America!'"

—ERNESTO QUIÑONEZ, Cornell University

"Like Walt Whitman, who found 'letters of God dropt in the street,' Harold Recinos finds in the 'sacramental gutter' the reliquaries and names of the exiled, banished, and broken by a hostile, almost fatal country. From his side of the Jordan, he sings in a braided Spanish and English—sometimes with a white hand around his throat—of tortured brown bodies and a contested notion of 'home.' He is a magus who recognizes and subverts the savage. He is a minister who attends to Bronx musicians, barrio residents, Breonna Taylor, and border crossers, delivering 'just the right amount of Spanish balm.' His is a blistering, prophetic song. He is unafraid, indefatigable, and necessary."

—BRUCE SMITH, Syracuse University

"With his own style of grammar and flow of language, with each poem Recinos steadily indicts America's racism and hypocrisy—reduces the lies of its political system and false prophets (more in it for the money and power than for God) to dust under the steady beat of the poems hammering on the anvil of his heart, his pain, his hope, his dreams—every kid in school should read this book. It's a must!"

—JIMMY SANTIAGO BACA, author of *Laughing in the Light*

"*After Dark* is graced by an urgent, persistent, liberatory voice that at one moment dreams of reaching 'all the way / to God's ear' and at another condemns 'the monstrous nationalist / leaving the White House.' Similarly, the poems in this collection honor 'a worker / who sweats for a petty wage' as well as 'dark children chewing / on bitter bread' and 'perishing on / this wounded earth.' *After Dark* makes clear that Recinos is a poet who has been gifted with an endless fount of benevolence and is guided by a faith rooted in love, humanity, and compassion."

—JEFFREY LAMAR COLEMAN, St. Mary's College of Maryland

After Dark

After Dark

Harold J. Recinos

RESOURCE *Publications* · Eugene, Oregon

AFTER DARK

Copyright © 2021 Harold J. Recinos. All rights reserved. Except for brief quotations in critical publications or reviews, no part of this book may be reproduced in any manner without prior written permission from the publisher. Write: Permissions, Wipf and Stock Publishers, 199 W. 8th Ave., Suite 3, Eugene, OR 97401.

Resource Publications
An Imprint of Wipf and Stock Publishers
199 W. 8th Ave., Suite 3
Eugene, OR 97401

www.wipfandstock.com

PAPERBACK ISBN: 978-1-6667-0994-0
HARDCOVER ISBN: 978-1-6667-0995-7
EBOOK ISBN: 978-1-6667-0996-4

JULY 16, 2021

Contents

Exile | 1
Border Walls | 2
The Building | 4
Compassion | 5
Holy Mother | 6
Dispatch | 7
Bread | 9
Costly | 10
Smoke Rising | 11
Fatal Country | 12
America Dreaming | 13
The Lesson | 14
Simple | 15
Yonder | 16
The Crossing | 17
In the Beginning | 18
Confession | 19
Memory | 20
Missing | 21
East River | 22
Belief | 23
The Gift | 25
The Journey | 26
Serious | 27
Settled | 28
The Moment | 29
Flat World | 30
The Nation | 32
Dream | 33

Black | 34
Public School | 35
Another Life | 37
Doo-Wop | 39
Hopscotch | 40
Sleepless | 41
The Bronx | 42
Morning | 44
The Stray | 45
Harlem | 46
The Border Guard | 48
Rumors | 49
Yearning | 50
Lie | 51
August | 52
Love | 54
Thorns | 55
Tears | 56
Heal | 57
American Dream | 58
After | 60
Creation | 61
Blasphemies | 62
Shine | 63
Gratitude | 64
Common Day | 66
The Bolted Door | 67
The Ed Sullivan Show | 68
Michele | 69

The Devil Walking | 70
The Walk | 71
Rent | 72
The Chosen | 74
El Mes | 75
Eating English | 76
The Quiet | 77
The Talk | 78
Breonna Taylor | 79
Not Afraid | 80
Titles | 82
Twisted Angel | 83
Absurd | 84
Sing | 85
Invisible | 86
Love | 87
Waiting | 88
Beautiful Ones | 89
Adored | 90
Breathe | 91
Fading | 93
Abuela | 94
The Café | 95
The Wall | 97
The idiot | 98
New Judge | 99
Plead | 101
Holy Water | 102
Vote | 103
Pity | 104
For Such a Time | 105
Day Turn Right | 107
Waiting | 108
Love | 109
The Vote | 110
Good News | 112
Sing it High | 114
School | 116

Solitude | 117
Phony | 118
Lost Things | 120
Welcome | 121
First Walk | 122
The Lowly | 123
After Illness | 124
The River Weeps | 125
Craving Eden | 126
The Alley | 127
Spanglish | 128
Smile | 129
Advent | 130
Waiting | 131
The Tree | 132
Confession | 133
Peace | 134
Road to Bethlehem | 135
Tropical Nights | 137
The Margins | 138
Holy Mother | 139
The Mountain | 141
Lazarus | 142
The Tyrant | 144
The Birthday | 145
Invisible | 146
Jesus | 147
Navidad | 148
Christmas Eve | 149
The New Year | 150
The Library | 152
Looking Back | 153
The Poor | 155
U.S. Capitol | 157
Potter's Wheel | 159
Skipping Heart | 161
New Day | 162
Cristian | 164

Pat | 165
The Rock | 167
The Pencils | 168

Exile

I live in exile beneath
the American sky that
looked upon my birth,
with people who think
life is always beautiful,
where sidewalk smiles
point to a good future,
in a place not found on
postcard images and
where children still sit
in crowded apartments
sadly, picking songs for
their own funerals. in my
country I live in exile, a
Brown man with forbidden
daydreams, a sofrito human
being who speaks Spanglish
to conjure visions from the
sky, the moon, rivers and
stars with the trusty words
my poor mother gave as a
gift. I live in exile without
having crossed the southern
border and my órale world
is sick with a fever made by
the bigoted blasphemies of
my beloved country.

Border Walls

I never liked the border wall
around English words sending
skin and bone children with
missing front teeth into cages,
making tired mothers on stick
legs run toward the American
made fence they think is safer
than villages fled under cover
of dark and declaring you are
despised to every newcomer
with the wrong religion and
color of skin. my heart pounds
every time I see the big Wall
with the words tossed over it
that shout alien like it was a
curse and hundreds of miles
of fencing praised like it was
God's own handiwork. I have
tried to put a different idea in
American heads, to teach the
Bible in Spanish, objecting
to the walling out as Frost
would say, expecting just a
few good Christians to say
the names of the poor who
move about in darkness and
get dizzy just looking at the
grotesque barrier that will
never mend a thing. I bet
you didn't know about the
children's height marks on
the Mexican face of the Wall,
that Ana came by one night to
see it standing a foot taller and

still making her slouched aging
mother smile. before I stumble
down the sidewalk, I will depart
from your English stone tossing
words and do my best to bring
down the Wall that will never let
your country skip across the
Jordan.

The Building

I saw through an open
window mangos on a
kitchen table, a box of
raisins resting on top
an aging refrigerator and
smoke coming from a
pan on the stove. I saw
a little girl from my fifth
floor window dashing to
the store on the corner
where she disappeared for
a long time. I counted the
minutes before seeing her
hurtling back to an old
tenement across the street
with ears of corn falling
from a brown bag. hours
of talk were released in
the kitchen about children
left motherless, resisting
the whip, caravans through
the desert, the density of
the jungle, the ghosts that
moved into the apartments
with us and without reason
the creaking wood floors
in the building learning to
speak Spanish.

Compassion

I noticed for the first time
walking in front of the old
Catholic church that the Irish
priest who said very little in
Spanish and who baptized more
than half the kids on the block
wrote his name on the sidewalk
next to Joseph, Tito, Lefty, Harold
and Rosa. Father Peres who gave
us bread to make it through hard
times tagged the dirty sidewalk
to say with old fashioned certainty
I will not walk away.

Holy Mother

you are the one who
carries the elderly on
your skin, who walked
hundreds of miles with
their secrets to another
country, who felt harsh
words beating against
your soul, who misses
the sound of Spanish
laughter and sees hope
in the brutal atmosphere
of this land of purple
mountain majesties that
is lashed to your fierce
grief. you are the one
who knows the way to
the places of grace that
named you in the image
of divinity. you are the
one who tells the world
of children taken from
mothers, toddlers lost
to parents and even the
devil laughing at tears
from them. you are the
one who lets centuries
of mourning cry
out to heaven!

Dispatch

I am writing to you from
an uncertain country after
saving my place in an Old
Testament story in a leather
bound book beside my bed.
you have no need for me to
tell you how often words in
my chafed heart inch their way
to the tip of my tongue and
then cramp up before levying
a thought about the present
state of things. Did I tell you
the last time I wrote that the
buildings tremble, the dogs
roaming the alleys where you
played handball bark now with
hoarse voices, sometimes you
can still see a policeman on a
mount ambling down Southern
Boulevard and the clouds seen
from the rooftops never have
stopped making faces. I spend
time trying to listen deeper to
hear you shout my name from
the other side of the river, to
lift from the past that sticks like
glue the childhood anxiety we
knew that spoke more English
than the braided Spanish in us.
I often find your invincible soul
crossing the haunted American
border and conjured by the faces
of a new generation of kids who
sit like we did on the stoop. I miss

you, talk about you often and find
myself still going to the market
just to inhale like we did together
when kids the sweet perfume of
the Puerto Rican coffee you so
loved.

BREAD

we have broken this bread
kneaded by fingers in a place
not far from here, in the heat
of days divided and with those
closer to the flesh of God than
the busted-up world will care
to admit. each tiny piece is a
windblown life with history
inside of it that is gobbled in the
name of the revolutionary peasant
who died in the company of rebels
long before we were born to give
us a little more life. perhaps, you
saw in the hands sharing the scraps
of dough or heard it from the mouths
of disregarded people that no one is
lost.

Costly

I never melted in the
American pot, shared
books in public school
and my mother worked
all her life for a minimum
wage. my father took an
English first name, never
owned a home, went to
school, and barely learned
to sign his name. they never
read Langston Hughes' poems,
didn't know a damn thing
about the Harlem Renaissance
or the Mexican artist painting
its life, but I tutored them in
this foreign English tongue
as best I knew. I spent time
in church trying to serve the
good news, marched with
bloody feet protesting inequality
and wonder when will America
find time to listen to my precious
colored world!

Smoke Rising

I often think about my father
with Indian blood, his dark skin,
black long straight hair, struggle
with English and hated for the
rest of his life in the USA though
he became a sailor and fought in
her second world war. he crossed
the border into the very country that
destroyed hundreds of thousands
of lives, was full of stories of loss,
Brown skin subordination and the
bleeding history he said of conquest,
colonialism, and slavery. he knew
where all the bones were buried by the
believers of enlightenment discourse
and pretentious Christian improvement
that engraved his world with no more
than white brutality and death in the
name of philosophy, theology and a
crucifying church. I often sat with
him when he was ever around to
weep for those eaten by empires of
pale flesh.

Fatal Country

there is a country
in the North built
under a vast cloudy
sky that removed its
doors. a simple word
like freedom without
explanation died and
the joyful sounds it once
sang are banished. there
is a country in the North
with quicksand floors for
strangers, where the gods,
stars, oceans, trees, flowers
and every passing breeze has
been renamed in English. there
is a country in the North sure
about not seeing, swarming
with imaginary demons and
breathing behind its very big
make-believe walls. there is
a country in the north bowing
to a God of hatred that rolls its
eyes to the poor, makes ashes
of the innocent and thinks
death for it will never finally
come!

America Dreaming

it started with a speech
full of gunshot words on
on the Ellipse near the
White House that many
slave hands built. a mob
excited by a white man's
lies and the world shocked
by the monstrous president
casting stones like the truth
never existed. his ravenous
crowd purchased the nouns,
verbs and sentences from his
fleshy face that levitated a
foul darkness unmet by any
light. it started with an
avalanche of after midnight
tweets for people who go to
hate instead of church and
utter words that are not nearly
human. it started with the
angry noise of insurrection,
the second he relieved himself
on a laurel-leaf, stomped Black,
Brown, Muslim bodies and
Capitol police to darken
heaven with more innocent
deaths. perhaps, we will stand
up to make it end, deny sleep
until the plague has ceased
and find our sweet America
dreaming again.

The Lesson

history was not explained
in Spanish, there was barely
a flicker of us in any of the
books passed out at school,
when we weren't junkies or
hoods, the contract historians
had us siting lazily beneath
trees or on city stoops. history,
for us I explained to them consists
of mourning at the Ortiz Funeral
Home and feeling a large old
white hand around our throats
while citizens shout English only.
history, I said to them is painted
barrio murals with the names of
dead kids like the water of the
East River that swallows Black
and Brown bodies each year. history,
I told these willfully ignorant writers
is the white man's chains that clatter
when we step and bitter prayers said
to the Nazarene who doesn't speak
English!

Simple

I laughed with the roaring
water breaking on the banks
of a Puerto Rican shore. I
splashed in the waves of a
South Bronx beach all the
mothers from West Farms
Road believed was bathed
with infinite light. I talked
the whole long Summer with
Joel about the love jammed
into the Aguacero botanica we
visited on Friday night with
eyes full of visions. I listened
to the stories about the way
freedom walked thousands
of miles just to see children
play and the elderly on the
stoop giggling at each other
trying to hug their very own
shadows.

Yonder

I sometimes wonder does
God keep watch on things
and is there still any value
in confessing hope in the
face of the revolting white
supremacy that makes us
colored people bleed? I am
not you see a pie-in-the sky
pietist and you may think me
a fool for holding on to the 20th
century dream shared by a Black
American preacher and a Central
American priest but I have reason
to think despite my stammering
tongue and the scars on our
beautiful dark backs that a day
will come for my beloved people
to loosen every bond and go
free! you see, despite the
ruthless malice of America,
I aim to live into the prophets'
dreams and confess tirelessly
on this side of the Jordan the
good news they so radiantly
exposed.

The Crossing

we walked extra slowly
approaching the border,
looking back a few times
to the land where flowers
weep at night to tell the
moon how they miss us.
we waited quietly for hours
with hearts beating much
too loudly for the crossing
and children standing on
rocks to stare across the
the phony line trying to get
a glimpse of their new world.
on the other side of the fence
a road was patrolled by Broncos
with shadowy figures in them
and when they passed migrants'
bones rattled, while the wind
trembled on both sides of the
Wall. the poor women and
children pushing north prayed
to find courage for the last few
steps of flight into a world that
Jews once settled after escaping
Hitler's Germany. an old woman
kneeling beside me shared in God's
world the poor and despised suffer
and they are murdered by wealthy
people who prefer not to be reminded
of their crimes. then, a little
girl announced birds had returned
to perch on the Wall, so we took it
to be a sign that passage was clear,
risked the river and began the crossing
into the hostile country.

In the Beginning

imagine, waking up in a
world that flings itself
into loving arms, has no
idea of strife, and every
whispered word, cry and
shout reaches all the way
to God's ear. perhaps, you
dreamed it last night and
today it is not a figment of
your imagination and it sings
like a bird on a tree.

Confession

we came into the sanctuary
whispering our faults and unclear
about kneeling before la Virgen
Sagrada like the other professed
sinners in the basement of Saint
John's Church that visited each
morning wanting to be saved. we
wore ornamental crosses and Saint
medallions around our necks though
were troubled about the wounds of
the dark-skinned man who was nailed
to the cross and the death of the Brown
fleshed Catholic Saint killed at the altar
while holding the body of Christ that
offers life to the poor. the nervous light
that came into the space considered sacred
did not cheapen Spanish speaking life and
in our confessional tongue we did not doubt
God could not live without us and understood
the plainest Spanglish brought from the streets
to the flaming altar and spoken by exacting
answer lips.

Memory

I left a lamp on in the
living room to return
to a favorite chair by
the window to read a
few lines that assure
me the world is made
of memories. I pause
on the page that said the
moon enjoys going on
walks and hiding behind
thick clouds like they were
God's own handkerchiefs
left in the sky for games.
I will sit for a while trying
to remember until the dark
that you are a traveler from
a Spanish world, a worker
who sweats for a petty wage
and someone who insists on
dreaming about the words in
in old church hymns.

Missing

sometimes I wonder
the long day where you hide,
what you hear and if you
see us tremble. the tortured
poor that ache to have a few
words heard are often tired
of searching for your light
and I don't think they have
much humility left to believe
what you said about the meek
inheriting the earth. I must
confess the cup with your life
sustaining gift tastes like grape
juice poured from a can and
the civil strife caused by violent
cops simply goes on sweeping
every one of us into the blinding
dark. mind you, I fear you have
not kept your promises very well
and your dark children chewing
on bitter bread are perishing on
this wounded earth. forgive me for
hearing lies when the church bells
ring, asking for more when reading
your book and holding our sick
children by the hand and demanding
you speak. I confess the birds in
the park ignorant of the for sale
ways of the so-called land of the
free have replied to our cares more
perhaps than you in that far away
place above where Spanish names
some say do not appear.

East River

I went down to the East
River around three a.m.
to sit on a splintered rail
road tie to wonder about
the fathers who had long
left, mothers wishing they
hit the lottery and kids
yelling in the alleys the
storefront preacher said
the world will end, soon.
I watched the stars going
out, thought about the
landlord who turns the
heat off in the winter for
days to save money and
remembered I would need
to wash my socks after
school. I looked around
for signs of any kind that
said kind Jesus was not
too far from the block,
close to Joseph's grave
and listening to every
Hallelujah sent his way
though it occurred to
me he just doesn't see
my face and like the
downtown crowd can't
speak Spanish. then,
slowly getting up I said
this is not Emerson's blue
river.

BELIEF

on an autumn evening
mother came home with
one grocery bag, a big
sack of rice, another
of beans and a six pack
of cheap beer. she said
nothing when entering
the apartment, looked
at her three kids on the
couch smiling, then
turned and then wept.
I only saw the face of
a girl that had already
lived a life too hard for
her years. I looked out
the fifth-floor window
and made out the church
steeple only two blocks
away and I heard words
erupting in my head that
said will you come? I sat
down next to my brother
with a bitter tear making its
way down my Nuyorican
face muttering will you come?
not a single word came back
in answer and I wanted more
than anything else to forsake
religion, then my mother called
us into her bedroom to pray on
knees before her altar of Saints.
I first spoke to her sweet God then
and had a long conversation with
the figure of San Martin de Porres

and decided to give the mute in heaven and his gang of saints a chance.

The Gift

I love flowers that open
when the sun is truly high,
the ones wet with the dim
morning dew, the kind that
tell stories from the night
before remembered by us
long after they are gone. they
remind me I cannot imagine
waking without seeing your
head on the pillow and feeling
the light of a new day heavy
on you. I will never stop loving
how you see the world's colors,
the warmth of your flesh and
knowing sweet darling with you
I have lived. I must tell how I
love the way you still sing lullabies
to the stars, cross wide rivers,
scale border walls and wait for
me.

The Journey

midway on the long walk
north pushing behind the
waves of sorrow it was
clear we were desperate
on this earth. dark paint
spilled from our tears and
we caught them in glass
bottles. we carried them to
fling on the border Wall
and to let children write in
big Black letters tear down
this hate. I would speak
for hours about the trip
but you already know
this piteous story crossed
the border even before
the guards took up posts.
I bet you have even heard
the cruel paternoster from
the bigoted people of God
that in the past sanctioned
slavery and today speaks
in loud English to condemn
again in every way Christ in
the strangers lynched on
USA trees.

Serious

the air, the parks, the trees,
the flowers, children, widows,
old veterans, noises, voices,
darkness and laughter all say
clearer than a thousand Sunday
sermons: we are here! in the
apartments the penitent old
country Catholics who prefer
to speak Spanish are on knees
waiting to hear answers, kids
sit in front of old televisions
wearing smiles that image the
happiness of heaven on earth
and the sound of music leaving
Papos third floor window blesses
time by reminding us life is a
great experience. a couple sits
on the stoop quarreling again,
but we suspect that after leaving
a dangerous life on the other
side of the border they are no
less in love. the two boys back
from shining shoes on the big
boulevard sat with the couple
on the stoops occupying the
step closer to the building door
and out of the blue one of the
boys asked: do you think the
dead can hear the things we
say of them? I overhear
the comment entering the
tenement, smile at the kids
and couple and feel a knot take
hold of my throat.

Settled

on walks like this after
dark down the long city
street like an old world
stoic, not bothering about
the purpose of these United
States, who deserves blame
for the terrible things of the
age, what time on Sunday
the imperfect church bells
will begin to ring, the days
of being homeless without
food, home or the simplest
sign of love that offers an
embrace, I confess there is
no reason to sob about never
going back home. tonight,
I laugh about the crumbling
walls that aimed to keep me
out, proclaim my heart to the
sacramental gutter that gives
me life and whisper beneath a
lamp post with names written
on it this is how my dusty life
settles.

The Moment

the moment came from
nowhere, it laid next to
us in the dark, it filled quiet
spaces like the soft wind
drying tears and without
uttering a word rested on
the muddy earth. time had
nothing to do but march on
while we stayed behind to
listen. I can only tell you
there was no language in it
and the things we take for
granted in life were shaped
otherwise.

Flat World

you may not believe it
but there are people in
the country living in
a flat world. they nail
weak thoughts to the
walls in their homes
and dark bodies to fly
buzzed trees. they are
willfully ignorant of
the greatness that waits
to be found on a round
earth. they fondly sing
empty hymns to a God
that never was and will
never truly be. detached
in their flat world, they
freely make up things,
look away from truth
hunched in the corners
of their flat hearts and
spend hours blaming
others for their faults.
you may not believe it
when I say these flat
people with thousands
of ways to throw off
light still wonder why
confusion in their flat
world is never solved
and why they lay awake
at night cursing instead of
listening to the unforgettable
certainty that the earth is round

and full of more color than
flat people like them ever
imagined.

The Nation

in the land where the memory of
the vanquished has been dismissed
for hundreds of years, the border
changed boundaries to trap us with
an exceptionalism that despises
Brown bodies. our children grow
up hearing tall tales that say this
land is indivisible and under God,
a place made one from many and
blessed, yet under this nation's God
inequality runs free and divinity is
too white for us to bend at the knee
with humble fidelity. in this land
that has always been home everything
is different from what fable makers
think, what the contract historians
write with glorifying lies melted
in ink and for the country that
carries us to the grave. we have
offered Brown flesh for hundreds
of years to ransom freedom and
slip these fucken chains wrapped
to our legs that keep us thoroughly
enslaved! one day, we will live in a
country that does not hate us and
sadness will not describe the places
we call home.

Dream

I dream with you in a tiring world and share your musing against every reason to hate. I dream with you for the sake of the river crossed, for the souls that have grown at the foot of the bleeding cross and the wretched hanging trees. I dream with you to hold on in this world till love returns and the broken no longer drown in tears.

Black

have I told you of
the beautiful Black
lives some people
curse and kill in the
name of the whitest
God ever to walk the
earth? have you said
the name of the man
born Black who was
kept by a crooked cop
from breathing? did I
tell you we know more
about tending wounds
and burying our dead
than you have answered
prayers? will you ever
speak up for equality, truth
and freedom and help
people full of loathing
see the human being on
on a lynching tree who
came to free the world of
sin? before you go telling
the world how much you
lament another Black life
crushed, lift the veil from
you white eyes, carry the
weight of our broken earth
and in the name of God
subvert today the traditions
of savage White power!

Public School

the desk in public school
where I sat had an inkwell
that oddly was never once
assigned with dip pens to
students. sometimes, when
a teacher asked a question
my eyes would drift to the
top of the desk and I would
stare into the hole to get a
good look at my imitation
Converse sneakers thinking
with my braided language
how to deliver a Spanglish
answer to the white lady at
the front of the room asking
with a smile what does Animal
farm mean? I had never even
seen some of the animals in that
Orwell book save on television
though Julia's mother had a couple
of chickens in the bathroom of her
apartment. I confess a love for
looking at maps on the walls of
the classroom and imagining life
in more countries named than barrio
kids like us would ever visit. you
know, public school taught me a
good many things and when the
books never bothered to mention
Brown people in America I would
shout counterfeit witness, then I
would be sent to the principal's
office like it was a place on the
school grounds for a last wish

meal. but, let me tell you my favorite
part of public school—free lunch!
man, sometimes that was my best
meal especially the sloppy joes
that came with seconds thanks to
the old Jewish women working the
kitchen.

Another Life

I asked God for another life
where it would not be necessary to
explain to my sons and daughters
why a white women ran her car into
a group of Brown skinned girls, why
the mothers on the block dress for
Mass wearing black and never stop
mourning the children delivered to
them in bags, telling them that the
Black, Brown and white faces they
see homeless on the streets belong
to human beings whose names are
known somewhere and still spoken
by someone like the Lord's prayer.
I asked the world's most renowned
mute to let me live in a world where
dark skinned kids can play on the streets
without being chased by white faced
and blood-shot eyed supremacists, to
read about Brown history in school,
to never be erased from the country's
civil rights history, to hear scholars
and preachers confess that their Latinx
kin were also lynched in the name of
white superiority. I asked God to wake
me up in another life in a society that
does not hate other languages, religions,
cultures, the color of skin or tell me in
thousands of ways your family does not
belong here. when I wake up in another
world, I want to breathe air fragrant with
the flowers my people harvest for penny
wages, eat the food they have cultivated
for a despising nation and sing with my

children in salsa rhythms while doves
patch the sky with the sweet words, free at
last, libre por fin!

Doo-Wop

I heard them singing harmonies
in the hall of building 1203, the
Bronx Puerto Rican boys who run
at the sound of shrieking police
sirens coming up the block, whose
mothers charge out of bed each
day to make an IRT train to jobs
that take them into night clearer
than the Saint John's Chrysostom
Church bells ringing sacred sounds
on Sunday for the living, the sick
and the long gone. they didn't wear
the characteristic fancy Doo-Wop
suit, were never bathed in applause
for their vocal harmonies and them
falsetto notes hit in flawless pitch
never attracted a call from a frantic
recording agent. I loved to hear them
singing above the noise on the streets,
doing little Anthony's Tears on My
Pillow, making the delicious sounds
that helped kids on the block jump,
run and play. when these Puerto
Rican boys opened their mouths the
world turned the color Brown and
people on the block I tell you saw
themselves whole in the light and
dark.

Hopscotch

he lived in the oldest
building on the block,
the one that got Christmas
lights on all its windows
and was stained by eggs
thrown by little kids who
targeted the ground floor
apartment door where the
old man with a whistle who
could not find wonderful in
the building never stopped
yelling damn spics, especially
when hop-scotch games started
up and the Puerto Rican girls
jumped rope. he never went
to the rooftop to see crouching
clouds speaking Spanish, white
stars welcoming black heaven
and people whispering the secrets
of life they carried from far away
places where that don't speak any
English. for years, he hoped things
would take a turn for the better and
that only meant the block would
be rid of spics and somehow, he
would cross the bridge into a white
pledged land.   I dared to speak
to him in my proud public school
English admitting what I learned
in the church where water was once
poured over my head that love for
strangers makes us whole.

Sleepless

there is an old woman at
her apartment window who
never remembers the time
of day. there is a mother on
the sidewalk followed by a
grocery cart smiling at the
kids playing with tops. there
is Jonny the cop exiting the
building to get into his new
Chrysler who forgets he was
raised on the block. there is
Carmen Julia sitting on the steps
after shooting dope on the roof
that her grandmother's dream no
longer can reach. there is Hank
the neighborhood drunk pissing
on a garbage can clueless about
dates. there goes the priest with
a bundle of flowers for the altar
of his church acting mysterious
for others to see.

The Bronx

when I heard Lefty was
forming a music group
and revealed the name
on the base drum that
read, *Sydney and the in
Crowd*, yes, I had to ask
these Boricuas: Who's
Sydney? the drummer
named Shorty was just
outraged and with words
that rose like balloons in
Central Park he declared
we think it's cool. I listened
to them play what everyone
called white rock like they
were discovering America
for the first time and
digging the beat. you know I
didn't hear a single note to
make the dead rise, the guy
on electric piano never touched
black keys and the brand name
drums crackled blows that
did not speak Spanish. the
singer began an original
song that never mentioned
that Puerto Rican kids were
prohibited from swimming
in the pools on the white
side of town or that Tito just
died in the basement from
a heroin OD. I whispered
out the window to the wind
my, my, my just this year

Mick Jagger released Brown
Sugar but Sydney who was
born on an island owned by
the Red, White and Blue has
missed every note.

Morning

in the quiet time of the morning
where the Saints wait in silence
for a word and no thoughts are
yet fully made, a red-winged
blackbird bounces on branches
searching with a turn of its head
for a forest. the day begins by
laying still though the cold church
bells are ringing in the distance to
turn on the lights in rooms yet so
full of sleep. I shall sit right here
beside the whistling tree until the
sun comes out or perhaps to wait
for the unseasonable time to come
lastly to an end.

The Stray

when it drizzled in the
early morning hours of
darkness and the streets
were near empty I walked
for hours to the tip of
Manhattan to sit in a big
doorless park just to stare
with poor barrio eyes at
Lady Liberty in the bay
and the working class
New Jersey shore. winos
slept on the battery park
benches, some holding
in their arms a leftover
pastrami sandwich half
tucked into a bag from
Delancey Street's own
Katz's Delicatessen and
I always imagined they
probably recited Hebrew
prayers for the treat. on
one occasion, a stray dog
came to me, I shared bagel
scraps with it, let my voice
cry out a simple name and
held its skinny outstretched
paw in my hands, then I looked
up at the stars just thinking in
that moment we had more
than most—funny, I whispered
into the dog's ear let's meet up
again for company and some
eats.

Harlem

the north end
of
Central Park
beside
Harlem
and El Barrio
is banging
with soul
and salsa.
when you
walk
that side
of
the world
you can
hear
stomping
and clapping
by the
time you
reach
the museum
hill.
with all
that
jive
and
life
in the
air
it's a
damn
shame
the

rest of
the city
won't
hear.

The Border Guard

what does a border guard think
after spending the day on his side
of the Wall? does he say I am glad
the tear gas canister did not hit the
toddler held by a mother, today?
does he turn on Netflix to catch
the latest movie release, find time
to play catch with children and
hug his USA born immigrant
wife? when his daughter comes
home to say she will take Spanish
in the new school year does he say
I have heard enough of it? does
he ever wonder about the women
and children condemned to jail
for crossing a border and think
about leaving behind the keys?
what does the border guard think
about freedom, the American dream,
cruelty to little ones and shushing
camp deaths? does he ever think
good does come from Nazareth
now the places on the other South
side of his Wall?

Rumors

we have eyes that
cannot clearly see
the fattening graves
and every wound
they bear. we have
a hand cupped on
ears that refuse to
hear purgatory is
just a piece of this
ill earth. and now,
we kneel to ask the
Angels with guileless
prayer to make us
visible to God.

Yearning

on the rooftop I see
how the moon drifts
and calls me to lean
into the wind while
imagining incurable
stories of love hiding
in every strand of your
long and restless hair
blown to me. in the
agitated world longing
for tenderness a quiet
moment like this on a
roof above the old city
sidewalks that are busy
sputtering things about
life, makes me confess
that eternity is entirely
knowable just like the
pulse within flesh that
carries a kiss.

Lie

Mirror, mirror
on the wall who
tells the biggest
lies of all? mirror,
mirror on the wall
look upon his face
and tell me is this
the look of dark
disgrace? mirror,
mirror on the wall
have you ever seen
a better likeness
of divinity? mirror,
mirror on the wall
when I remove the
make-up from my
face am I not the
best, sexiest and
most accomplished
president of them
all?

August

I went
for walk
in a
wooded
park,
the sun
burning in the
heavens,
hope
floating above
the tree-tops,
birds
cradling their
young
and
the scent of
nature
unable to
keep
from
stirring
the silence.
for that
precious time,
I withdrew
into
myself
uncertain of
what to
find,
pounded on
the stony
parts of
my heart,

then
in whispers
confessed
I was
too small
and
bent in
the
world
for such
regal signs
of grace.

Love

I kissed your lips that prayed next to me until doves descended from the tops of trees and danced beside us to make us children. your silky hair without care was blown by a cooling breeze and we smiled at strangers who strolled in the park without time and like a rushing river embraced in moments of first love. I can only say here we are so very close to everything and sinking into the tenderest parts of life. all the other lovers who have been taken into eternal silence admire us from the stars and quietly we look up at them in the kindling heavens. in the perfect time I confess life is too short on time and precious words.

Thorns

the world knows how
they make us gasp for
air, blame us at the
border, create hell for
us on earth and separate
our families in brightness
of day. the world knows
about our useless begging
for life, it hears the names
of our mothers hollered,
the endless cries of children
in darkest night, the words
in pretty speeches that make
it a crime to speak Spanish
and not have white skin. tell
me how can we pray in this
Christian nation, talk about
Bethlehem or smile with the
people who hear the church
bells ring from the comfort
of a pew and comprehend
nothing. what we most fear
is your Ivory towers with
white feet, your wells that
deny our thirst, the absence
of celestial wisdom and your
white supremacist hate. but
I tell you the world knows our
dead will never be forgotten
and we will always breathe!

Tears

the wet thing rolling down
my cheek Madre Sagrada,
this warm trickle of soul,
drops in all the places that
have grown dark and on the
English streets that leave us
without breath. standing up,
I weep when looking into a
day full of shadows strolling
by just to pick up the light to
carry it far away from desert
sand that still adorns these
Spanish speaking rags. I
can't tell you why the wind
brushing against my face
makes us weep or why the
scent of flowers in the old
barrio makes our eyes moist
with sweet brown tears, Madre
Sagrada. But I must ask you
today dear Holy Mother what
remains after they call us
spics?

Heal

you have been traveling
a long time by foot, bus
and train. in the journey
language changed, the
first words of your life
are in English, children
who play on the streets
laugh in it, the nowhere
block is vastly invisible
for it and the tenement
sheltering every shadow
and dream for you is now
a place to gather memories
before letting them fade
beyond rescue on this
new land. I will sit with
you for a little while and
wait tonight for the sidewalk
to crack open and see water
rise from a spring that will
quench our thirst and wash
us into a new world.

American Dream

what you call the American
dream only set some among
you free and came with land
grab thievery, every slaves'
grisly scars and the wicked
sight of innocent blood lapped
up by the white village dogs.
what do you know of our
colored dreams, our bodies
weakened by the masters
whip, the profit made in
the fields, the orchards, the
factories, the countryside
and cities from human beings
often dangled for diversion by
white hands from big old trees?
what do you know of the people
born in this country denied a
place in your history books who
harvested the fields, built the
railroads, highways, bridges,
streets and over centuries have
suffered to offer the finery of
your American dream? when
will you finally admit it was
Black, Brown, Yellow and Red
humanity that gave its life to
set your land free! who made
America, like Langston and
Brother Baldwin, I cannot say
any plainer but people beautiful
like a pitch Black night, Brown
like the mother earth, Yellow
like the warming sun and Red

like the blood that runs in every
earthly creatures veins!

After

the days have lengthened
more than ever imagined,
we sit apart, open windows,
stand on balconies, listen
to songs from the favorite
list that helps us let warm
tears tumble in the dark
and hear ourselves say just
a little longer and we will
reach the same old crowded
tables in the café, just a bit
more time until we raise
cups high shouting, cheers
and surely by winter's chill
we will cast aside the dreary
way of life and come together
to lift drinks in the name of
a simple human touch. soon,
I think many of us will write
hymns about the thousands of
ways we tried to hide from the
sadness and the unbearable loss
of others!

CREATION

I saw the morning open
its eyes in the city full
of belief for the start of
a new day. the colors on
the street were dim and
cleaning ladies, laborers
and pushcart workers that
climbed into it were still
tired from yesterday's hard
work. I saw old women
coming out of tenements
dressed in black for the
local church they believe
helps them see the world
a little more clearly. by the
time I reached the steps of
the subway station for the
ride downtown it was clear
if Eve had walked with these
people she would have given
the world a different name.
the morning invited you to
recall the old lessons about
being created from clay and
destined one day to be dust
though it occurred to me that
the imperfections in creation
pointed to haste in God's own
work.

Blasphemies

I walked by the cemetery
where in the quiet darkness
souls fell out of bones long
before heading down the river
of the dead and they caught me
unaware like a sock with a big
old hole in it. before saying the
last good-bye, they asked why
the living made in whiteness
make a home of violence? I
watched them being taken away
by strong gusts of wind and with
the memory of every dark body
beaten and lynched and all the
luckless believers in old school
human decency shouted, I do
not understand this madness
but what is certainly overdue
is what the church calls a second
coming—see for yourself!

Shine

in a yellowing summer
morning Cano gathered
his shoeshine box and
church borrowed chair
to make his way to the
Southern Boulevard. he
passed the wall where Shorty
was shot, the candles left
for prayer by his mother
and paused in front of the
aging house of spirits where
twice a week, old people said
the Rosary in Spanish and
gossiped about keeping each
other's secrets. he set up his box
beside a parking meter with
torn pieces of paper pasted to
it announcing meetings at the
local public school organized
by the people who deal with
unspeakable events. the boy
reached into his pocket for
holy water collected in a little
bottle from the local Catholic
church and poured its protecting
drops on his head. despite being
thousands of miles from God
he admitted being ready for a
good day of polishing shoes for
a whole buck.

Gratitude

music poured out the
apartment door with
a cheap stick-on photo
of the Pope wearing a
smile next to la Virgen
de Guadalupe. the vast
hallway of the tenement
collected the noise that
echoed all the way up to
the fifth floor where God
was getting drunk with
the domestic workers.
when the insane Angels
come roaring across the
sky above rooftops in sweet
chariots they will not hear
the hypnotic strings of
Barber, nor pause in the
middle of a gallop for the
emotional reach of Mozart
instead, they will hear Willie
playing salsa on his big old
trombone and the Jewish
cantor living on the first
floor singing in Spanglish
like it was his first language.
by the time the moon comes
out the whole damn block
will be celebrating Joey's
release from jail, giggling
with his little sister and
laughing with his mother
whose smile for the last

six months was painted
on the alley walls with
a cross beside it.

Common Day

the desperate slipped
out of the dusty building
into the shadows and
they whispered. I heard
them say how oddly
light bounded across
rooftops confusing the
hungry with murmurs
of the good news that
is drunk with heavenly
kisses. I listened to
the desperate who were
losing costly dreams
speak softly saying when
will the bright descend
so a clear-cut moment
can slip inside of them
leaving nothing the same.
I wondered with them
does trampled humanity
ever make appearances
in God's dreams?

The Bolted Door

the moon begins to disappear
in the lighting sky, flowers
are eager to open and well
kept are the secrets spoken
last night about the people
lost on the way to the border.
later in this long day, we will
find mothers' faces in the
clouds and fresh-stepping kids
in mourning who paint messages
on the vast blue sky to confess
death is not the end of life. to
speak truthfully, we will recall
the things taken away from us,
the dreadful days on English
speaking streets and the silence
of the First United Methodist
church with arms too short to
throw around us. today, like
many others the wicked will
be out squeezing the sweet
life out of the American justice
creed and directly into the
hands of the hateful God they
pimp—but we will not vanish,
shut up or lose sight of the
heavenly keeper of dreams
who promises to unlock all
doors!

The Ed Sullivan Show

because there was no receptionon
the old picture box, I grabbed
a hangar from the closet in the
crowded bedroom that slept five
people, pushed it into a tiny hole
where an antenna use to sit, then
sat back with others in the room
waiting to see the Ed Sullivan Show
clearer than the ice cream truck
parked in front of the building.
slowly, clear images appeared
on the TV screen to offer an hour
of magic and redemption that only
the really, really big show hosted
by Mr. Sunday Night could ever
deliver. stiff Ed looking like an
undertaker put Vaudeville in
common laughter and made my
Puerto Rican mother scream in
the fifth-floor apartment from her
first excited look at Elvis and the
Beatles who made sweat run down
Ed's nose. the vibrant picture came
into the dark room from the old
TV and it occurred to me that Ed
was commanding like Ezra Pound
said the wild beasts for a nation
in change. the television gathered
snow for a few minutes and when
the man unsuited for television
came back on to announce the
appearance of the Supremes I
smiled big.

Michele

Michele do tell your wacky
story for all to hear that
transgender Marxist wish
to overthrow the government
and end the traditional family.
Michele do tell what prophet
in the Bible wrote the lunacy
you read. Michele do tell us
of the tea you share with Beck,
Limbaugh and the conspiracy
theorists that love to stir the
pot that brews the zaniest
ideas to make our heads just
spin. Michele do tell is this
latest piece of silly ass shit not
just like the time you claimed
slavery was an institution that
bred mutual respect? Michele
do you remember the nation
believed you were the funniest
thing that ever happened to
presidential politics—and here
you are still telling over-sized
jokes with a touch of bible
to make us laugh!

The Devil Walking

the words are likely still
echoing in your ears that
the man from paradise lost,
filled with a granite theology
of hate, who has never been
heavy with shame or kneeled
in a godly church or felt the
deepest wounds of a Black
soul was willed to the White
House by God. the preachers
who prayed for bombs to drop in
the Middle East, while applauding
the brutality of cops will never
tell a finer lie and their believers
like cattle in a fog will last until
the great slaughter, while the rest
of us going half-mad will think
the traitor to the truth and hero
of the criminal high-class has
left us in the name of God a
sick country dressed with the
Devil's sizzling parts.

The Walk

I asked you in the middle
of an abstract conversation
about the meaning of prayer
whether or not you noticed
yesterday's wind does not
leave a trace when it flows
through the streets, enters
a church or simply brushes
the hair from the eyes of
young mothers walking kids
home from school. I could
see your weightless soul in
that moment searching the
neighborhood and most certain
the breeze like the words offered
by the living to a divinity not
seen would return. we walked
by a small group of Puerto Rican
girls laughing on the sidewalk for
whom everything was possible,
heard the dim sound of a Spanish
speaking radio coming from an
apartment window and became
breathless with laughter by the
time we reached the corner when
you said no one can know what
gives between the wind and your
Catholic God.

Rent

we live
on
lent
breath
that
is the
same
today
as
yesterday.
we
cough
speeches
in
city
parks
and
claim
every hour
good
or
bad
our
own.
we live
in a
world
without
borders
one
body
and
hope.
we live

in a
country
with
no
image
of
God.

The Chosen

where will we live after
the roof that once covered
our heads from the blazing
Spanish Sun is gone? the
fading days of that other
life is tucked in a closet
now too small for all of us
to dwell. we spend each
day pushed around like
fugitives, listening to the
words that deport us and
explaining to the kids who
sucked their first breath of
American life in the city
hospital of the poor that
their history here is more
silent than stones. you may
not believe me but the rank
smell of death crossed the
border with us and it lives
in the same neighborhood
white faces never visit. the
old men and women around
here without a country pray
to find life without fault and
those of us born here hold on
to specks of dream dust!

El Mes

because you may not have
noticed us in the last five
hundred years walking on
this land collecting your
star spangled wounds and
making your identity more
whole, we raise the flame
of freedom and expect you
to say our names. tell me
have you noticed us standing
in the fields, working in the
factory, taking care of children,
cutting grass, building houses,
roads, bridges, hospitals
and schools. tell me have
you noticed us in science,
medicine, education and
justices of court, and even
astronauts writing letters
back to this old earth.
perhaps, you are familiar
with the way day and night
we lament how you detain
our children, keep us in and
out of jail and tell stories
of a God that defends
imagined rightlessness
for any people with dark
skin.

Eating English

you have never seen us
eating English words
before they have a taste
of us. it takes a little bit
of time sitting at a table
in the kitchen dressed in
unwashed clothes having
porridge before dashing
out the door for a day at
public school. you have
never walked with Emi
and Tito the fifteen long
concrete sidewalk blocks
on which they pretend to
be America's budding English
teachers and carry just the
right amount of Spanish
balm in tiny pockets for a
day of hurt. I guarantee that
when you eat these words
with us they will go to your
head in an entirely new way
and help you find our voice
already inside of you.

The Quiet

every day in the moments
of silence the sun shines
above our head shedding
holy light on all the stories
we tell. every second we
cling to love in precious
life in the places it has left
a trace. so much depends
on silence, the stones that
wait to speak, the strangers
without words, the long night
before a dream, the falling
stars that skip across the sky
and the moon that floats with
light. perhaps, the quiet will
hang around today, thoughts
will calmly appear like words
printed on the quiet pages of
a book and we will confess the
calm as nothing more than
supremely true.

The Talk

let's sit in the park to
talk about the outrage
burning streets in cities,
years in public school
with strange books that
admit nothing wrong
and the memory of the
people never mentioned
by a teacher who inspires
us to live. let's sit to talk
about great love stories,
Borges' poems, Allende's
magical tales, the vision
of Mistral, Marquez's
novels and the congas
beating in Crotona park
while marchers pass by
singing passionately for
hundreds of others gone. let's
sit to talk of bearing witness
like an apostle to the stark
realities of a country engulfed
now by the fire next time.

Breonna Taylor

we will say your name
on the steps of courts,
the judges' chambers,
and every station with
errant cops. we will tell
your story on the nation's
streets, paint your face on
municipal building walls,
and remind an indifferent
white society your Black
life matters in any spot of
light. with your beautiful
dark face leading the protest
march we will rush to demand
justice for you from the evil
cops, the Jim Crow courts and
this fictive white nation that
is glad to make us bleed. today,
we will disturb white peace to
say not one more ethically
innocent Black death!

Not Afraid

we are not afraid of
your knife sticks on
our heads, they can't
do more than make us
bleed and they will never
strip the life from us
despite making us not
breath. you will never
make us fear to take
the nation's streets to
demand the birth of
justice, equality and
peace that with every
march and vigil brings
our Black and Brown
lives a little closer to
free. we are not afraid
to speak of dreams, to
call you out for your
single-minded hate, to
accuse the good folks'
silence and the wicked
ways of whiteness. we
are not afraid to say on
sidewalks, the churches,
the courthouse and the
very halls of Congress the
words you speak with piety
are full of ugly holes and
everything you see burning
comes from the vast sorrow
you thought would simply
dry us up. we are not afraid
to protest until all the clocks

stop ticking, the church bells
stop their hypocritical ringing
and we begin singing about the
sweeter things of life that make
us equal and finally free!

Titles

the teens with no titles next
to their names have tagged
the walls all over the block
including a line that says
Oscar Romero Ora Pro
Nobis. they have their own
way of talking to these dim
times by putting up words
that shout back. in the late
autumn not even the dark
morning and the pale light
from the sun can shut up
the mouthful of words they
use to condemn the people
with letters behind their names
that lie about freedom and
democracy, while making
damn sure it doesn't mean a
thing for Lela and Black
kids.   they have plans not
to spend life bent down to
make others rich and I met
just yesterday a whole bunch
of them insisting that even
the wind without a title for
itself and never university
trained would speak for all
their needs and dreams!

Twisted Angel

I was sitting on the stoop
minding my own thoughts
when a twisted Angel
from the church around
the block came to me
saying don't bother to
come to the church where
people count wrong in
other lives. I nodded my
head to let the heavenly
visitor finish then said
it takes a herculean effort
to spend time in the peace,
joy, milk and cookie space
with the troubling on the
streets. I did not want to
hear a thing about the
distorted readings from
the Holy book, especially
with honey slowly pouring
from the cracked bricks on
the filthy buildings where
my beautiful wretched
people live. before the
twisted Angel left, I said
hedging my bets God must
be with the darkest people
walking by the stained glass
windows of that old church,
so I will stick with my insane
devotion out here and laugh
with friends about the spiritual
escape artists in church saying
the streets are full of wrong.

Absurd

the contributions to history
that have been made by us
have not been reported in
white time. the daily crisis
that splits our lips and leaves
us unable to smile along with
the stupid chatter of colorblind
teachers, ignorant politicians
and otherworldly preachers
confirms the diagnosis that
we are America's terminally
ill. in the world where you
yet live the questions the
simplest people ask stumble
against all the old bookshelves
and you just stand there in
a dim light shrugging your
damn white ass shoulders. I
wonder what you will say
when we are gathered up in
the loving arms of God and
you are asked why did you
do nothing for the stomped
people on earth.

SING

I sang the morning with
halftone notes by using
the Psalms familiar to the
bruised who hear stones
talk. the strangers coming
out of the buildings heard
it and thought it was a very
good way to pray for a new
day of dreams. I wanted
them to take the melody on
the subway, to Babylon on
the far side of the city, the
reading rooms at school at
every place where love is
not for sale.

Invisible

as the 21st century marches on
like people confined to the
barrio never existed too little
earthly light shines on Spanish
speakers. in the old fragrant
tenements the residents busily
reinventing themselves begin to
put on their masks before heading
to their cheap jobs. here people who
give each other hope, where every
ticking second is an act of love, and the
overlooked accomplices of paradise
have taken up residence without
permission. they cannot say when
their stories will be taken into account
or who will heal the thousands of wounds
inflicted on them by those ignorant of
the requirements of God. loathed and
battered my invisible Brown people on
these streets can tell you magnificent
truths your foolish white ears should
hear!

Love

I have loved you longer
than speech, in countless
manners known in this life
or any other to come, by
way of thousands of stories
told and not yet known in
one culture or another, with
my heart beating joy and even
sorrow, with hands holding
tightly to this moment now
and in every style imagined
before time ends. I have loved
your sacred Spanish name, held
you close with no more than
open eyes that looked at you
standing beneath the stars and
enchanting night. I have loved
you in the short days of life, for
the ways you braid your hair, the
sensual sweetness of your lips, the
memory of flowers you painted on
a hand and sweet bread eaten together
from a basket.

Waiting

do tell me who was that
God that heard the cries of
the enslaved, crossed into
earthly life and got lynched
on a tree? do tell me has
this divinity taken any time
to read the words in the big
book you read, seen the short
script written on bottles and
tossed out to sea, wept with
the disillusioned grandchildren
of those who crossed the Red
Sea, listened to the heartbeat
of lovers on the other side of
the Jordan still waiting, talked
with the widows holding wax
candles in dark churches and
sat with robed priests enjoying
the morning song of birds? do
tell me on the booming nights
of insurrection, the streets that
chant with uprising, is the object
of your prayers, the sweet Lord
whose name you call still there
giving birth to another world of
precious freedom? do tell me
how much you care for the poorly
dressed, the hard working, the
loathed and your own creators
beautiful Black flesh? I'll wait
but do tell something of the old
truth that raises the dead!

Beautiful Ones

the newspaper was left to rest
on the subway seat and the news
in it reported stories about the
block afflicting us. we will
repeat those stories hundreds
of times each day and ride the
subway to the old garment district
warehouse to work and search
desperately for a glimmer of
the Lord's repairing bread. by
the end of the year any truth
in our eyes will be beaten out by
the hard labor required of us in
a country named in English. in
this time that perfectly rejects holy
light you can't blame us for wanting
to grab stones to throw at those among
you who loathe us.

Adored

the years not imagined
gone so swiftly whisper
to me about your sweet
voice and the warmth
of your breath that hints
of the mysteries of lost
paradise. with my hands,
I grasp the rushing wind
trying again to zestfully
hold you in a conjured
moment that leaves me
with songs for the silvery
moon. when the world is
dark and cursing me, I
hear your voice and forget
why I weep now that you
have gone.

Breathe

strange, they think
everything Black was
rejected from paradise
and heaven has great
big signs at the front
gate saying no Blacks,
Mexicans and dogs are
allowed here. their white
English speaking streets
with new levels of fear
and loathing eat us. they
forget, the flowers and plants
laid out on the lawns of the
pretty houses were planted
by large Brown hands that
haven't held the caged child
that people breathing easily
in guiltless worlds just never
notice. today, I will skip down
the city streets holding beautiful
Brown hands, dance on cracked
sidewalks illuminated by dark
faced smiles, hold a towel for
sweet Lela washing her Spanish
only grandmother's feet, then
begin to walk another round of
protest miles with the people who
built railroads, bridges, highways,
houses, schools, streets and that
fenced up White House at Black
Lives Matter Plaza. before the
sun goes down, I will smile with
the people who crossed over the

bullshit border waiting to hear
God's trumpet blare to bring
down the Wall.

Fading

the mural on the corner
wall has worn away and
the faces Henry painted
no longer watch over the
local ruins. in the alleys
with gathered shadows
the kids play all the same
and the girls jump rope in
front of the fading master
work a museum will never
curate. the white families
that lived on the ground
floor fled several years
ago and I sit now with a
bunch of Black and Brown
faced kids saying the block
is beautiful.

Abuela

there is room in the
night to take in quiet
streets and sit just to
imagine the unknown
relative. I never did meet
my grandmother, no letters
came to the apartment,
found no pictures of her
pressed into a draw for
nostalgic review and no
stories about this woman
was ever spoken. I never
hesitated to imagine her
with long black hair, dark
eyes and skin. I was certain
she was so beautiful that
had she visited New York
in winter the snow would
melt. often, I thought of
taking her hand after stumbling
out of public school and rattling
things in Spanish that despite
the words she would really not
understand. I only learned
the name of one, my father
never leaked the other after
so many years away from his
indigenous land. I confess in
the end it did not matter for abuela
was less real than heaven so many
people believe certain. perhaps, it was
best for her not to hear us sunk into life in
a big city with odd English names and
rubbing stones that could not speak.

The Café

I lean back into the chair
at the café while a waiter
dressed in black pants, a
white shirt and thrift store
vest rushes to the table
behind me like he is trying
to make a train. my eyes
bounce around the near
empty room taking in all
the primary suspects who
are guilty of refusing not
to experience life in a time
of hope and illness. I recall
sitting in that space when
crowds roared with laughter
and noisy voices tossed words
across the East River to say
no one is home. I sat with two
poets from the Puerto Rican
diaspora one night and they
removed the lid from a jar
that kept years of insults in
it that were thrown from high
offices in government, respected
academics, pastors and priests.
they wanted to set adrift the
vile sentences packed in the
recycled glass container that
following a week of reflection
Pedro labelled pure bullshit.
they looked at the tiny church
across the street from the café
observing the unchanged lives
parading in front of it like they

were voices crying in the wilderness
in a country that outspends itself
to slaughter the innocent.

THE WALL

stop the wall's
full 2000 miles
of hate. wherever
it is up let it tumble
down on bitter white
heads like in Berlin
when a U.S. president
said, "Mr. Gorbachev
tear down this wall!"
stop the wall with
border agents on
monstrous watch,
vigilantes on patrol
pledging allegiance
to white nationalist
ways, old Miss Betsy
sewing confederate
flags and the court
pastors full of cheap
grace. stop the wall
ripping open hearts,
erasing others from
the face of the earth
and raised by a country
that replaced freedom
with bigoted bulllshit.
stop the wall blocking
the light from heaven
shining like God's own
scars on this impious land
the world knows despises
justice and love.

The idiot

the idiot spits
obscenities at
the world from
pink lips on the
most peculiar
orange face. his
vacant eyes, big
belly, tiny hands
and forward lean
is flatly rejected
by the world that
cannot endure his
stench!

New Judge

nine justices you see
are making decisions
in unenviable times and
for a future that will
decidedly bleed. a
great woman passed
on, leaving behind her
giant steps, footprints
to equity, justice and
hope and never a knee
on a civilian neck. some
years ago, I had the great
honor of sitting beside RBG
at the Kennedy Center for a
panel discussion on race and
ethnicity in the criminal justice
system. with clarity she spoke,
the dead rose from their graves
and Black and Brown humanity
warehoused by wealth cheered
and said her name. today, we
are saddened by the willful rush
to appoint a new justice in the
name of one nation divisible,
who will store in secret rooms
the equality and justice meant
for all, in the name of her shallow
CV, imminent legal foolery and
wilful ignorance of the imagined
Eden that makes us whole. stony
will be the road to trod for years
to come but we will follow the
fierce steps nonetheless of our

dearest RBG and recall the very precious pages of American history this woman wrote.

Plead

there was a time not
long ago we sat together
and never surrendered
to the deepening dark.
there was a time when
civil strife did not
reduce the idea of
American democracy
to muck. there was a
time when words had
more promises for us,
they untangled malice,
lead us in long justice
marches and flowed
like a mighty river in
the languages of the
great big and colorful
earth. there was a time
when leaders did not try
to sell a broken world, no
one was forced to wear it
like a hideous scar and
we talked about beloved
community like a thing
of this earth. Lord, to
live hopefully again is
what we plead here and
now!

Holy Water

besides Sunday there is
very little to remember
of the visit to the pious
churches where eager
members volunteer to
make coffee hour pleasing
like the sound of choir
voices. after all the altar
calls, the people appear
no nearer to the God who
freed slaves. how painfully
true that so many citizens
with Spanish names in these
United States feel like aliens
here. after Sunday services,
the people with the nationalist
ideas that began on Plymouth
Rock will practice a week of
cruelty in a Black and Brown
wilderness until the next time
bored preachers speak in the
name of a barbed wire God.
after worship, they will sit and
eat and some will believe Holy
Water will somehow wash
them clean.

Vote

we mourn in America
according to the second
hand of a ticking clock,
the sobbing above the
hard ground where our
beloved slipped into the
dark and while the devil
runs for a second term
with the abyss humming
in our ears. we have no
time to complain, no reason
for sadness to have its way
and slowly with every
remaining breath and
before another week of
setting suns, we vow to
see the quivering hate and
grotesque image of democracy
labor toward the liberty that
aims to break all the new and
ugly chains.

Pity

whoever said God is white
must have never held a Bible
in hand, read stories from its
pages and never understood
God is far more than White,
Black, Yellow, Brown or Red.
God is more colorful than a
rainbow that follows a storm,
darker than the earth beneath
our feet and the witnesses say
at the execution bleed red from
any angle seen. whoever says
God waits on them to grant
eternal rest will either shout
for joy or weep when they
finally come to rest in the
arms of a dark man named,
Jesus!

For Such a Time

for such a time as this we
read the biblical prophets,
listened to the marchers
scream, prayed beside the
grieving mothers, sobbed
with family and friends,
found comfort in words
that declare justice. for
such a time as this we
have been made to break
every chain of hate, to
overcome the inventors
of holocausts, to find in
the big sky the chariots
from heaven sent, to dare
in perilous walks to chop
down those lynching trees
and angle history toward
the precious will that died
for justice to be done and
on earth a promised land
of mercy, justice and ever
lasting peace. for such a
time as this we rise away
from lies and we are not
afraid of the grotesque eyes
that stare to tell us to stand
back and never throw these
stones. for such a time as this
Mandela, Martin, Romero,
Chavez, Tubman, Angelou,
Malcolm, Bonhoeffer and the
innocent victims with unknown

names illuminate our steps
and nothing in all the world
will prevail against us!

Day Turn Right

I hold on Lord but the
little while sometimes
makes me tired. I cry in
the dark Lord, where no
one sees me and I hear
you say hold on change
is coming soon. I pray
on with my freed slave
heart trembling about
centuries of violence,
the rivers of bleeding
from the dark skinned
and my heart is often
overcome with sorrow,
then I hear you say hold
on things are gonna be
alright! I wonder Lord
how long your children
can go on with slanted
life, fighting back tears
and trying to keep dreams
alive, then you shout out
hold on its gonna be alright!
I cannot even put words on
paper to you now without
sobbing Lord then once again
I hear you say hold on cause
everything is going to be alright.
Lord, hurry and make it so!

Waiting

in the advent season
under this bending
heaven when summer
birds have flown far
and the cold streets
are nearly deserted,
we wait for the stars
to break the chilling
silence. on this old
earth, the children
wait in daily play,
the widows watch in
dusty churches, the
strangers light old
lamps that seem to
brighten the road to
Bethlehem, and we all
wait together for the
sweet sound of the
crying infant to fall
upon our lowly ears.
in the long wait, we
strain to see the perfect
child of God whose tears
are gently wiped away
by a young mother who
allows a few to gently fall
on our parched lips! in the
strong cold of winter, we
wait for the child Angels
name and for the coming
prize of deliverance to justice
and all the places of peace.

LOVE

there are too many
ways for those who
delight in pure hate
to harm others. but
the only way to feel
the goodness of life
is to love your foes,
embrace dear friends,
cherish sweet family
and turn our hearts
in the direction of
heaven. today, I
will pray for those
who persecute the
ethically innocent
in the name of the
unwavering hope
that I still do not
fully understand.

The Vote

in the hours left for
counting, we sit in a
subway car making
the trip downtown
discussing how the
dead from the block
would have voted and
whether such an act ever
overcomes the history
of genocide and lynching
we carry in the pocket of
pants bought in a Jewish
store downtown. the train
pulled away from Simpson
Street Station, where the
service workers speaking
rapid Spanish boarded and
you told me that the eagle
clutching thirteen arrows
and an olive branch in its
talons has seen the streets
in our mothers' countries
lined with bodies and it
may even weep now when
it flies over our America to
drop pamphlets that read
have a nice day! after the
Jackson Avenue Station
the subway made its way
into the dark tunnel
and we recalled that
Tito's father did not
vote to learn English,
help his sister sneak

across the border or
sing when the roll is
called up yonder. we
fell silent for about
five minutes then said
out loud maybe this
time it will be different
for people like us.

Good News

we let the weeks run
us down while these
United States grew
smaller and the man
in the White House said
no one deserves the
world more. we are tired
of throwing punches
in the air, crying in
each other's arms,
praying for change
in church and finding
sliced pieces of life in
the company of the
hurt. we can finally
say something of a
revelation is on hand,
dazzling news has
come our way, two
vivid faces poured
light into the dark
and the wicked days
to announce change
like a winged horse
from a better world
is on the way! I can
say to you the world
we dreamed is coming
back and doors will be
placed on the big and
ugly Wall. today,
we can thank heaven
for not taking an oath
to cages, walls, the

racist church, its political
party and the economy
that rapes the earth. today,
we dare welcome hope
and shall stay vigilant for
freedom to welcome the
the huddled masses on
these shores.

Sing it High

for all the world to
see the toxic man
with never a plan
is trying desperately
to recast reality away
from the statistical
truth. for the rest of
American history the
global imbecile will
live with the new brand
name in a matter of
days he earned, loser.
the fake president with
his long public record
of defeats never in
his untouchable life
imagined the humiliation
the world with cymbals
and shouts celebrated
in his baneful name. yes,
wake up you sleepyheads,
ding dong the wicked man
is gone. the man with all
that unappeasable need
for affirmation, adoration
and attention from willfully
ignorant supporters and
friends was fired for never
doing anything good and
especially serving himself.
through the world the joyous
news has spread the wicked
man is on his way to the world
where all the cursed goblins wait.

ding dong the wicked man can sue
a sandwich if he likes though
numbers like science will not
bow to his bullshit and the
world will spit on every one of
his wretched lies!

School

we all went to Orchard
Beach first on the Pelham
line train and then on a
city bus. we talked about
the English class offered
at P.S. 118 where a very
nice White teacher could
never understand why the
Puerto Rican kids in his
composition class wrote
Nuyorican stories about
the Perez grocery store
called a Bodega or little
Willy playing dominoes
sitting on top of a milk
crate, while experiencing
the world in the Spanglish
chi-chi schools of education
dismissed. we talked about
getting bad grades for telling
the teacher we think and
write in a Nuyorican way,
colored like the great earth
and dark like the people
evaded on the street by the
English teacher's White
world. we are a whole lot
less free than the White male
teacher standing at the front
of the classroom though
that does not keep us from
passing notes in Spanish
saying a lot about the hellish
American dream.

Solitude

I wandered the city alone
to the lake in the Manhattan
park, sat pensively beneath
the largest tree, watched the
feathers on small birds that
came to drink and dance in
the breeze and spent hours
doing nothing required of
me. I befriended solitude,
wrapped my arms around
her, experienced her like a
moth clinging to a colorful
flower and promised never
to let go. that afternoon not
a thing mattered and the
life packing words in my
throat rested as I inhaled
the fragrance of my city
that pushed its way East
to West in the park before
becoming silence.

Phony

the image of scorned
children driven out of
their cities to end in a
cage, beyond the reach
of Holy Bible stories,
altar candles and the
Psalms of lament fed
weekly to parishes that
never experienced what
Moses heard on the
mountaintop leaves
very little on this land
with thousands of churches
to reach me. you see, in
my world we pray for a
hand to reach down from
heaven to comfort them,
to point us to the hundreds
of children lost by men
and women who said these
kids are too dark to be a
bother for love or for the
decent Christians in the big
steeple churches that just
will not defile Whiteness
with tears for these Brown
and uninvited guests. foolishly,
those who think submitting
to the doctrines of faith and
spitting indifference at the
crying dark faces of caged
Spanish speaking kids are lost
on the road to Bethlehem and
a full of the wicked spiritual

arrogance that the cruelty of Herod alone would think very delightful!

Lost Things

I have searched for something
lost, cried steadily for it long
after suffering, tried to find it
in the old buildings, the familiar
sidewalks, at the altar of an aging
Catholic church, buried in a Staten
Island boneyard and on the fragile
streets of this old city. often, I
sensed it near healing the broken
hearted in barrios across this wide
country named by many tongues,
on the crowded subway rides to work
in a warehouse on the whiter side of
town, in the barefoot steps of strangers
strolling the Great Meadow in Central
Park and even in the rambling words
on the side of tenement walls facing
the sun. at night, when sleep visits
the places resting in the dark, I lay
awake to ask God questions about
lost things, family long gone and to
make sure nothing wanders through
the room after being hidden deep in
the dark.

Welcome

the streets are never
noiseless and people
with crying eyes sit
together on stoops to
talk in Spanish about
troubles. the cracked
steps of the tenement
weep with them and
the landlord who only
speaks English cannot
understand. they begin
whispering that Jesus, the
border crosser grabbed
Maria by the hand, parted
the river like Moses and
walked her all the way to
New York singing slave
songs in Spanish like it was
his maternal tongue. I could
see in their eyes they were
not showered with revolting
stones and for the moment this
strange new land bubbled up
in them like a new welcoming
home.

First Walk

what was it like to dream
for the first time freely on
earth, to cross mountains,
seas, blistering deserts and
dense forests? What was it
like to wander more than half
the earth to be startled by the
beauty of many tongues, the
places where different people
got their names and colorful
terrain where nothing could
be taken away?   what was
it like to sit beneath the stars
on land that was not a country,
to lay our lips against weary
children's cheeks who smiled,
to bathe in many rivers cared
for by clouds and to see God
dancing in them? on the long
walk across splitting land did
the first people get a glimpse
of Angels basking in the sun
with the creatures of Eden? I
can imagine creation pulsing
in their ancient veins like a sign
of the mysterious and luxurious
difference God did so smartly
dream.

The Lowly

the winter season is closing
in on us making the mercury
in old thermometers plummet
like falling stars. the darkness
enlarges its hours, church bells
ring familiar carols, the penitent
think about peace on earth and
the wicked fail. the faint sound
of sweet children singing Christ
is near is carried by the wintry
wind from the border and like
a fine heavenly choir they set
our steps to Bethlehem and to
the place on earth where truth
was shouted from heaven in the
stench of a stable that was visited
by Holy Sages who humbly
prayed. this winter season will
walk us into the mystery of the
the undocumented God taking
infant flesh who comes to walk
the earth with us.

After Illness

it has been too long since
strolling down Broadway
to sit at Duffy Square in
the middle of billboards
and lights that shout louder
than ticket hawkers in the
park. Times Square is barren,
the costumed characters that
posed for pictures have all
gone, a few grocery stores
stay open like the church to
sell food and drink and the
naked Cowboy still plays
his guitar in the middle of
the street and gives away
money to the homeless that
never left. heaven pity the
empty streets, the people who
shelter below the canopy of
shut theaters, New Yorkers
standing beneath damp street
lights feeling empty and to
you pleading for a cure. one
day soon, the playhouses will
gather us up in their arms, the
streets like in a dream will see
the sun rising over Manhattan
and this ghastly virus will be
carried by thoughtful Angels to
met its end!

The River Weeps

you reach the river that
has run before you were
a child, the water that
is never still, the torrent
dividing two shores that
holds ancient secrets and
separate lives. you have
known its muddy waters
from songs about it starting
in the San Juan Mountains
and reaching the Gulf of
Mexico, looked upon the
water and seen reflected
in it the ancestral faces of
your people displaced by
violence from its shore
and now you come with
children to sit beside it
until nightfall to make the
legendary crossing you
hope will end a dangerous
trek and provides you with
a life worthy of your very
ancient soul.

CRAVING EDEN

an unaccomplished man living
off an inheritance and a truck
load of borrowed money, who filed
six bankruptcies, has five children
from three marriages, denounced
by his sister and condemned by
a niece for being a bully and a
cheat was president of the United
States of America. history will
never hide his shame, it will be
recalled by the memory of over
half of a million dead, violence
against the innocent and repeated
treasury raids. no matter where
his party tries to bury it in years
to come, it will hang in the air of
cities, be written about by historians
and the little school kids and haunt
the corridors of Congress and the
idea of democracy until time ends.
imagine, American was led by an
idiot for four years, called the truth
fake and made so many white people
hungry for an apocalypse and driven
by hate!

The Alley

last night, I walked down a
dark alley thinking who to
accuse for the suffering left
on these streets, the orphans
who will never know they
resemble their mothers, the
beggar who plays a violin
beneath tenement windows and
waits for human kindness to
wrap coins in newspaper tossed
to him. I walked the back alleys
for quite a distance beyond the
reach of the bright moon promising
to leave a reflection, past the lonely
voices in the tenements and hoping
there was truth to the idea simple
silence too heals. I walked telling
myself a sleeping God in a barrio
not found on any map is having a
bad dream and will wake up soon
murmuring something however
hesitantly about the interminable
time of waiting coming to an end
and the world complete with the
possibilities of life hitherto not
imagined.

Spanglish

on Avenue D,
the chatter
on corners, music
played in grocery
stores, the dull sound
of old city buses and
barking neighborhood
stray dogs happen en
Spanglish and God
speaks it, too.

the lovers walking on
the avenue, the people
weary with the blues, the
stoops crowded with kids
who dream the day long
and even the graying priest
expel edgy days, grief
and sadness darling en
Spanglish.

Avenue D where the end
of the world comes round
at midnight and runs at
sun up is the place God
settles, old domino players
say while sitting on milk
crates older than Joey, just
to talk loud and long en
Spanglish, baby!

On the first warm day of
winter, come on out and
hear it yourself!

Smile

the Loisaida Avenue
bag lady who scattered
ashes in the Tompkins
Square Park on a chilly
Autumn morning liked
to stand on the corner
collecting petty change
from the barrio poor.
often, you could find
her in the park by the
East River the meek
living in the projects
on Avenue D could see.
no one knew her name
and she sat for hours to
watch the charms of the
muddy water waiting for
something to happen like
after you get sprinkled by
a priest with Holy Water
in a Christmas Midnight
Mass. the cadets from the
police academy ran along
the East River often by the
bag lady though collectively
blind when they came along
but she would block the path
and give them a flash light
smile.

Advent

the first Sunday of the
winter month arrives
with wonder for ordinary
life when people around
the world look to a slender
infant and see in the innocent
face announced by an Angel
the milk and honey that helps
them cross the Jordan again
and again. laborers watch
within, domestic workers
with hope, the activist with
candles lighting up the dark
and those who weep in the
long night for the promises
to come at God's daybreak.
in these expectant days we
strike up the music of old
earth, we kneel with a mother
who gave us God in flesh, we
confess with the wise and the
poor giving heaven thanks
for this world good enough
to receive this glorious and
saving frailty.

Waiting

we hear the restless
pacing in rooms for
days on end like it
was a rain dance calling
on the reign of God to
come and confirm the
pleads of prayer. all this
frantic walking up and
down is meant to reject
the idea of being alone in
the cruelness of time that
appears only to know divine
absence. I see people talking
about unspeakable things,
how pointless to seek and too
anxious about passing things. I
quietly listen to fine sentences
demanding a hearing with truth
and it occurs to me the first and
absolute reality is in the flesh, in
love with us, and some say in a
Savior born poor who cannot live
without our broken world. perhaps,
we can go on chanting hope into
the long night, shake away the tears
and even wait just a little longer for
heaven to draw near.

The Tree

when Christmas neared
we walked the boulevard
to see the sparkling pine
tree, while the whistling
wind plowed through
the city with tantalizing
gossip. we stared at the
nativity scene to find God
in its silence and signs of
new life. sometimes, we
talked briefly of the birth
narrative in Luke and how
our sacred Maria pondered
in her heart like our mothers
in the Bronx. on the way back
to the fifth-floor apartment, I
recall carols being gently sung,
Puerto Rican faces enchanting
God and though we had no gifts
or even a tree there was plenty of
joy and the apartment windows
were adorned with colorful festive
lights!

Confession

we paused to hear them speak
of good, to tell us in plain English
dreams are not illegal, to condemn
the heart full of hate in the stringy
man rejected by his Jewish family
for delivering horror to the migrant
innocent, to hear the nation begging
for bread and to condemn the White
House den of thieves. we waited
for the leaders of the places where
the candles burn to decry the flat
lies in the name of the God of life
who takes the beaten, broken and
put down to uplifted life. who
among them remembers the long
walk from slavery in Egypt, the
flight from Herodian violence and
the holy call to make the crooked
straight? tonight, we will leave
the window open to listen to their
confessions!

Peace

we carry the message of
love in dark seasons, repeat
the word like prayer, while
our lantern eyes search the
street corners for signs of
peace. we walk the avenue
humming tunes about the place
beyond the stars come to old
ground, the way it lights the way
through tall grass and concrete
paths to the constant carols
the Christians sing. perhaps,
after the noise of the season
ends and the New Year begins,
we will see the invisible history
of peace and those promises of
divine good will for men, women
and children on earth.

Road to Bethlehem

last night, I listened to the
wind pounding the window,
cars rushing down the dark
street and wished to have the
ability to fly to the detention
cages along the border unlock
them and bring those children
home. once back, my impatient
hand would dial up the priests
I know in the lands that speak no
English and we would find the
broken-hearted mothers and fathers
with open arms and tears that for
months raced into helpless prayer.
perhaps I will see them go free
in the new year, find some in the
marginal villages where I have
been included by the oldest love
on earth and experience like never
before God's mercy still at work
in the world. last night, I quietly
wept for my people and these kids
that have spent their lives trying
to find freedom and were thrown
in a cage and it occurred to me
I have nothing to lose praying for
a plague to come down heavily on
the architects of suffering and the
lovers of crucifixion. all night, I
could not sleep thinking about
being up with the mothers of lost
children who read bibles until the
words collect in their dark eyes like
bloody tears. I heard them wailing

against America's cruel God who
is deaf to the despairing cries of
Brown children garrisoned by border
guards in a heavily locked hell. last
night, I opened the Bible to read a
few lines from Luke about God in
the flesh and wondered why Christians
in this country look away from strangers
and keep Bibles shut?

Tropical Nights

in these cities, we can only
imagine the tropical nights
left on the other side of a
long border, the volcanoes
spread across El Salvador
with odd clouds above them
and flowers growing on the
winding paths children love
walking. in these northern
cities, we lament the villages
left, the forest smells now no
more than memories in a memory,
the beloved cathedrals where priests
offered the hearts of the poor to
the Mother of God and prayed at
the altars adorned by widows with
the flowers risen from volcanic ash.
in these northern cities, we still dress
our children in rags, our hands are no
less wrinkled, calloused and stretched
like church step beggars. in these northern
cities, we hide in the shadows to speak
Spanish with the frail voices that make
the new face of the American poor and
nonetheless we are not too weak to hope
for new possibilities in life!

The Margins

the sun slowly rising
reminds me that I am
against people making
threats to lynch God's
sacred human beings,
slogans that invite you
not to think, rich white
men full of insecurity
and dressed with sin and
Christians believing bullshit
about the poor in their pretty
affluent church. today, I will
declare to more than a few
my love for God made flesh
in a bastard who promises to
turn me inside out and help me
hear the cantankerous bells that
swing all day in the overlooked
slums.

Holy Mother

the Puerto Rican girls
know Maria who gives
birth to God in flesh

beneath the heavenly
stars in a place no swankier
than the basement apartment

where Lela's kids go cold
in winter. they pray to her
with Spanglish voices and

after the lights go out in the
crying apartments, they look
inside upon the suckling Jesus

with gentle love and in a tumbling
world they know so well they
see his light. the local church

has never sent a priest to visit
the teen mother with her infant
baring her breast and telling

the Puerto Rican girls through
Lela's voice about her days of
hiding and the night an Angel

came to say you shall be the
mother of God. the infant drinks
from the merciful bosom of the

unwed teen just like each of Lela's
kids the Puerto Rican girls know
by name. in their heavenly Spanglish,

these Brown girls sing praises to the
bastard child from whom grace in the
world will flow.

The Mountain

last year, I traveled by air
to the warmth of another
land to heal my third degree
burnt soul from the cruelties
of your American English
world. I sang hymns on a
mountain with an assembly
of revolutionary women for
whom love come to earth
from heaven is not simply
a manner of speech. last
year, I held Brown hands
that belonged to war widows
eager to tell me their Christ
kissed land is home for people
of corn like me. last year on
that mountain top, I was more
certain than ever that heaven
may not be far and I confessed
wherever darkness stalks me
and leaves me with no footing
these revolutionaries on earth
will call me home by my full
name.

Lazarus

you had nothing to leave
me save a fake silver ring
picked up with a clock and
calendar at the dollar store
at a time when we did our
best to make the most of
every moment in the Bronx
parenthesis everyone swore
was life. we talked that night
in slow motion about the old
men playing dice on the curve,
Lefty who ran numbers, Manny
who had more wounds than
Lazarus from shooting dope
thousands of times in his long
shipwrecked life and the first
time in school that you heard
about the infamous American
dream. I put the brand-new bible
a bishop gave me after ordination
with a poem about you between
its pages in your coffin, dressed
you in my only suit and looked
at you in final judgment before
closing its lid. I am still as you
often said *people like us* who long
for the absolute mute named God
to say a word about kids hanging
on the corner, young mothers all
worrying on the stoops and dark
people who arrive and leave
crippled just the same on this
section of earth. I am tired of
praying and thought perhaps old

fashioned sobbing would get a better
hearing in heaven—let me know!
hey, I still have the cheap old ring
that was taken from your lifeless
finger and given to me by a doctor
at the city morgue where I picked
you up for one last time. you know,
the crappy ring like a Bible warms
my hands from time to time!

The Tyrant

the toppled days are near
the end and the stupefied
yet parade the streets in
search of limbs to break
and heads to split. there
are no signs of a merciful
God in their march and the
message their tyrant brings
leave trampled bodies the
respectable party leaders do
not see. when he complains
dishonesties in the middle
of night the innocent everywhere
die and the crematoriums fire
up the dark like crosses blazing
on a hill. this world of white
savagery unfurling proud boy
flags carried by goose-steppers
coming for the men, women and
children with dark skin will never
make us give-up in the hours of
discontent or bend when facing
such afflicting hate in our own
land.

The Birthday

I see you today an
imagined first Spring
with the wind gently
carrying your voice
from evening here to
light thick somewhere
with peace. I hear you
whispering to me the
secret of life in the name
of mystery and sweetest
things. in the dark, I find
your words carved on my
heart, those that were once
carried by the keepers
of important things, and they
tell me you made ancient
earth itself spin with the
fragrant and seducing love
that in me for years has
dwelled. so, my everlasting
darling, happy birthday now
and forever!

Invisible

the nation deserts
me several times a
day when it dreams
of everyone across
the land without me.
I shout in Spanglish
for a hearing though
it is clear the history
made by my people
has fallen away like
dry leaves. the trees
we planted are still
here, the same birds
look after them and
I can tell you their
Spanish names and
if you give me some
time describe to you
the memory and taste
of each word. at times,
I look up at the moon
that watches so many
cry and then it leaves
saying perhaps on this
land dreams end but I
resist leaning into that
stiff truth.

Jesus

one chilly winter morning
Ana was rushed to Lincoln
Hospital where she gave
birth to a little boy. on the
block, we jumped up and
down at the news and spoke
this child will have bullet
proof skin, his dark eyes
full of hope will leave his
teachers speechless and
in the school spelling bee
he will deliver the names of
every beggar in the troubled
city. the brown boy was named
Jesús and he gave his mother
the power to speak and smiles
crossed the faces in the building
with exiles. on the streets, in the
schools, and in jails, this sweet
child grew strong and he pleaded
for kindness in the world.

Navidad

this year, the advent bells
are weak, the stain-glass
windows pose quietly in
the dark, the altars are not
lavishly decorated, the sun
scuddles across the sky and
the quiet pews are recalled
at home with the story of the
child come to earth with the
good news of God. this year,
the caroling softly sings news
of Bethlehem, for those alive
with hope and too many seen
no more and silently we look
up at the stars giving thanks
for the full weight of sublime
mercy, justice and peace that
to us is given. this year, we
bear witness nonetheless to
mighty God that looks again
at us living in a world too dark
then brings us over to faultless
light and love.

Christmas Eve

we cast laughter adorned
with light into Christmas
eve, break bread before
children are hurried off
to sleep, contemplate in
the quiet room the old
knowledge of a Pine tree,
wrap the last-minute gifts
signed by the rising star
of love that has enchanted
all of our hearts and in a
suffering world lean into
the gracious hours of the
Holy Mother's labor that
grants us a live boy who
is fluent in every tongue
on earth and points the way
to places of everlasting justice
with peace in God's own
world.

The New Year

the parting year
has left
us inquisitive in the
dark,
longing for milder
times and dreaming
the world well
again.
the near faded
year has settled
within us
and
New Year bells
bicker
about miracles
delayed.
so long old year
and
all your
restless,
best
and unthinking
days,
let the curtain
down
on your hours,
gently part
into your night
and let us
turn
the page
with
hopeful cheer
to face

a better
patch
to
come.

The Library

in the New York City Library
where lions at the front door
wear masks and the steps are
not busy with the settled, I sit
content to turn the pages of a
book that talks about the year
moving slowly into the future
and the streets not alone. a few
readers are in the high ceiling
room hunched over the pages of
their favorite books, even in the
darkest season, in love with the
quiet time of learning and sunk
in a world of their own that is
untouched by the hacks of bad
news who avoid reading rooms
like meaty faced politicians the
truth. today, I am arguing with
the well employed theologians
who write elegantly about divine
union in creation, questioning
their confusion of an all-white
God in a world without foes and
offering instead the idea that God
made flesh is the beggar at the
gate unhappy with the fumbling
mess we have made of the whole
wide world.

Looking Back

on the last day of the
year the old woman
on the block are out
in the night gathering
moon light to help us
see clearly. though
poor and full of stories
about the country that
never loved us, we are
glad to open our mouths
to call it home, to drink
water from a tap, breathe
English speaking air, feel
these ordinary multilingual
days, have children learn
their way in public schools
and smile about nationalist
fairy tales that imaginatively
overlook us. in the new year,
we will line up words in our
Spanish speaking throats that
will inch their way out into
public life in broken English
just to talk about things other
than the sorrowing that followed
us from distant shores, we will
kneel in church tonight promising
to laugh and find things beautiful
in places known, never seen and
wherever on the quaking earth
our feet dare wander. on the
last day of the year, we will
gather dreams in baskets, mix
the moans of the innocent with

laughter, make jokes about the stupidity of hate and live for the sake of love each day for years to come!

The Poor

the poor are familiar to
me on these streets. we
have walked the avenues

together passing the fancy
buildings imagining life
in them with kids. you see

there are too many of us in
the world, we are barely
remembered but always there

like breaking day. the poor
are in the Holy Book making
its steady word about doing

righteous things, we are furiously
mentioned in its pages that some
say were inspired by God and yet

we are easily forgotten. the poor
are supposed to keep their place
in the world that loathes them

and before the wicked rich who
fear their lives yet need every
inch of their limbs until they go

to graves. on the corners, in the
alleys and sometimes even in a
church, I have prayed with the

poor for daily bread for those
broken and toiling here on earth
where the deliberate will adjusts

to cruelty, evades understanding
from heaven and thoughts about
having pity on the meek.

U.S. Capitol

I spoke to the wind
today about Judas
coming down the
dusty street to give
us the kiss of white
supremacy while his
friends dance around
strange fruit hanging
from the ugliest of
trees. I heard shouting
from the building over
about Brown deaths
never in the news and
Black lives that White
Judas keeps saying just
don't matter. I saw a
rippling lynch mob in
the Nation's Capital,
goose-stepping haters
of the lost cause, pissing
on Puerto Rico Avenue,
spreading feces on Black
Lives Matter Plaza and
parading with Auschwitz
worded shirts through the
corridors, offices and the
very chamber of liberty
in the Capitol building in
the name of a White House
with doors tightly shut to
truth. I spoke to the wind
about the poison in white
Judas and asked do you
think the letter of the law

will mean a damn good
thing for the politicians
forced to shelter in place
to take an elderly lunatic's
parting shot?

Potter's Wheel

I have felt the suffocating
hold on my throat, the kicks

in the stomach, the judgment
of people in plain white skin,

the bloody lashes uttered by
deporting words and entirely

bad examples from a public
untraveled in our Spanish

speaking worlds. you can't
imagine how many obscene

words I have coined in two
languages that made their

way across the vast sea to
settle here. in every rock

and stone, I have searched
for signs to help me call

this land home, to hear the
centuries old echoes of the

voices saying your father
cut his braided hair and

wept and you no matter how
mixed are good enough for

God. I have sat at the table
with exiles to talk, laugh

and weep, felt caressing
hands gently nudging me

closer to some truth and
stretched my soul beyond

limit to find evidence
for the claim we are all
made from the same
clay earth!

Skipping Heart

I have been cursing for four
long years with words more
foul than my bilingual head
ever imagined. I did ask the
good Lord to never mind the
babbling brook of lewdness
shouting in my Latinx head
but I refuse to take a single
curse back. I do pray that
inauguration day turns into
a time when no white man
will lynch dark people still
and the monstrous nationalist
leaving the White House will
find his way soon to the rotting
souls in the netherworld!

New Day

on this long awaited
day we greeted the
sun eager to tell it

the different story
we carried like an
overburdening cross

the length of these four
years. we woke today
full of prayer, breathing

hope, weeping for the
the missing and catching
the fierce shouts of history

remade though dark hate
still looms in the air until
together we bring it to its

knees to beg forgiveness.
today, after a threatening
storm, we watched the

celebration, the stories
great women bring to
keep the nation whole,

the dreams that loathed
human beings made when
conquered, dispossessed,

put in chains, beaten, lynched
and finally set free. today,

hatred could not find a place

in the heart of the nation's
second Catholic president,
Dixiecrat politicians were out

of lies and blue eyes were
removed from the flag to
have it wave the colors that

still sweep across mountains,
are in every valley and stretch
from sea to sea. today, we

took the first step toward
truth and removed masks
of grief to begin the long

walk to heal a broken nation,
hold the wicked accountable
and claim the dream that keeps

us struggling to make a more
perfect union, again.

Cristian

in unkind winter
wrapped for cold in
a mobile home, after
seeing snow for the
very first time on a
day when sleeping
trees too came wide
awake, a little boy
was swallowed by
the cold. not a single
eye was dry for the
child who at age eleven
was the oldest he would
ever be. on the richest
land on earth, a little boy
was slaughtered by the
cold in the state a Ritz Carlton
vacationing politician calls
home.

Pat

I hold
dear
the
trip
into
the villages
and
mountains
in
El Salvador
and
today
the
children
in the
places
you
visited
tell me
the
smudges
on the
hospital
windows
are their
kisses.
I would
love
to
come by
to open
a
window
so in a

flash
you
could
feel
the
warmth
of their
colossal
love
for you
equal
to my
own.

The Rock

the rock has been on
the forest ground for
innumerable years, who
knows even beneath the
sea or hosting whistling
birds on its stone back and
teasing eyes in search of signs.
you know, after days of doubt
a rock dripped water in Horeb
tasting ever so sweet and still
I see it flaunts the knowledge
of things and the lost mysteries
of silence. you know, the rock
will quietly find ways to speak,
to have us lift our eyes to the
sloping hills, the alien shores and
faces brilliant with hope, love and
tenderness. the rock in light and
darker time will matter to this vast
earth and I suspect to the insistent
curiosities of belief as well.

The Pencils

the children fell awake this
morning to face the hidden
news made in the dark hours
of a passing night. they trip
down long flights of stairs
on the way to school with
hair modestly combed and
clothes from the Catholic
thrift shop staring at the buses
and planes high above their
heads going to the elsewhere
places they will never get to
see. they walk the ten blocks
to the school where learning
is free, hear devoted teachers
butcher their names and after
taking Spanglish size breathes
reach in their schoolbags for
pencils that have secret lives
and hold them tightly in dark
little fingers ready to make their
mark.

www.ingramcontent.com/pod-product-compliance
Lightning Source LLC
Chambersburg PA
CBHW051100160426
43193CB00010B/1263